FOCUS ON GEOGRAPHY

T0024892

Focus on
Indonesia

Linda Barghoorn

A Crabtree Forest Book

Crabtree Publishing
crabtreebooks.com

Author: Linda Barghoorn

Series research and development:
  Janine Deschenes

Editorial director: Kathy Middleton

Editor: Janine Deschenes

Proofreader: Melissa Boyce

Design: Tammy McGarr

IMAGE CREDITS

Shutterstock: Gerdie Hutomo, cover (bottom); Pvince73, p 5 (bottom); INDONESIAPIX, p 7 (bottom), p 25 (top); Sukarman, p 8 (bottom); oko SL, p 10 (top); Matyas Rehak, p 11 (top); Uud N. Hudana, p 11 (bottom); Mohammadridwan, p 14 (top); Creativa Images, p 15 (bottom); Fedor Selivanov, p 16 (top); Cahya Ilahi, p 17 (top); Yavuz Sariyildiz, p 18 (top); Widya Amrin, p 19 (middle); Kamar Mini, p 20 (top); Sony Herdiana, p 21 (top), p 33 (bottom), p 26 (top); ImajiePro, p 21 (middle); Hairul Ashter, p 21 (bottom); Fresh Stocks, p 23 (top); Dhodi Syailendra, p 23 (middle); raditya, p 23 (bottom), p 39 (bottom); Kristina Ismulyani, p 24 (bottom); ZYV, p 25 (bottom); Hasrul Eka Putra, p 26 (bottom), p 30 (middle), p 40 (top); Leonard S, p 27 (bottom); Eo naya, p 28; akuditaputri, p 30 (top); I AM CONTRIBUTOR, p 30 (bottom); Bastian AS, p 31 (top); Dede Sudiana p 31 (left middle); BK Awangga, p 31 (bottom); Jekahelu, p 32 (top); phectography, p 32 (middle); Novie Charleen Magne, p 35 (top & right); priantopuji p 35 (bottom), p 37 (top); wisely, p 36 (top); Anges van der Logt, p 38 (middle); Oka diana, p 38 (bottom right); Khairul Effendi, p 39 (top); Adi Haririe, p 40 (bottom left); Rumbo a lo desconocido, p 40 (bottom right); Dicky Sutjiptohadi, Bastian AS, p 41 (top & bottom); p 43 (top); Masmikha, p 43 (bottom); Adil Armaya, p 44 (top); dani daniar, p 45 (top)

Wikimedia Commons: Smeeton Tilly, p 17 (bottom); Leiden University Library, p 27 (top); Van den Brink/DLC, p 27 (middle)

Public Domain: Universiteitsbibliotheek Leiden, p 19 (bottom); Enrico Strocchi, p 39 (bottom left)

Crabtree Publishing

crabtreebooks.com   800-387-7650
Copyright © 2024 Crabtree Publishing

Hardcover	978-1-0398-1523-0
Paperback	978-1-0398-1549-0
Ebook (pdf)	978-1-0398-1601-5
Epub	978-1-0398-1575-9

Published in Canada
Crabtree Publishing
616 Welland Avenue
St. Catharines, Ontario
L2M 5V6

Published in the United States
Crabtree Publishing
347 Fifth Avenue
Suite 1402-145
New York, New York, 10016

Library and Archives Canada Cataloguing in Publication
Available at Library and Archives Canada

Library of Congress Cataloging-in-Publication Data
Available at the Library of Congress

Printed in the U.S.A./072023/CG20230214

Contents

Life in Tana Toraja

A series of **remote** mountain villages are scattered across Indonesia's island province of South Sulawesi. Around these villages, villagers labor in lush, green rice paddies, which have been carved into the hillsides. This area is home to the Toraja people, whose name means "people of the uplands." Until the 20th century, these **Indigenous** people were largely isolated from the **colonizers** who arrived centuries ago to take control of Indonesia's rich natural resources. Their way of life has changed due to contact with settlers and tourists, but many still follow ancient beliefs and traditions.

Cultivating rice has been a core part of Toraja society for centuries. The practice involves hard physical work. The men of the village prepare the fields, plowing the land and building **terrace** walls. Women plant, care for, and harvest the rice by hand. Traditional songs and dances are performed to celebrate the annual rice harvest. Rice is eaten at every meal. In fact, a local saying, *"kalau belum makan nasi, belum makan,"* means "if you haven't eaten rice, you haven't eaten."

The **tropical climate** in the province of South Sulawesi lends itself perfectly to growing rice. The crop is grown in small, flooded fields called rice paddies.

The Toraja live in uniquely shaped wood houses known as *tongkonan*. In a society in which everything is shared, even houses are passed from one generation to another.

Animals are a symbol of wealth for the Toraja. Families strive to have as many chickens, pigs, and water buffaloes as possible. Water buffaloes are sometimes used to plow the fields. Chickens roam freely, while pigs are kept in small pens and fed until they are fat and ready to be slaughtered for food. Pork or chicken dishes—cooked in bamboo over an open fire—are popular.

Isolated from the outside world for generations, the Toraja developed a strong sense of community and family. In this place, village members are expected to share what they have—food, clothing, and even personal possessions—with everyone else. Any money that is earned must be shared among the entire family.

Tourism in Tana Toraja opened up in 1970 and became increasingly popular. However, tourism development has sometimes clashed with the Toraja way of life.

Indonesia is an enormous **archipelago** that spans the equator, stretching from Southeast Asia to Australia. It is made up of thousands of islands—so many, in fact, that no one has an exact count. Some islands are heavily populated and **industrialized**, while others are remote and **uninhabited**. Many don't even have a name. Only named islands are officially recognized as part of the country.

The country's population is the fourth largest in the world. Because of its enormous size and varied geography, it hosts a diverse population of people, languages, and cultures. More than 270 million Indonesians, made up of around 1,300 **ethnic groups**, make their home here. They speak more than 500 different languages and **dialects**. While Islam is the dominant religion, all major world religions and a number of Indigenous religions are practiced in the country as well.

The islands of Java and Sumatra contain a large portion of the country's population. The capital city of Jakarta is home to more than 10 million people. Its architecture, food, and culture reflect its colonial roots and its status as a modern economic center. However, its position on a river **delta**, which lies largely below sea level, puts it at risk during extreme weather such as **typhoons** and **tsunamis**.

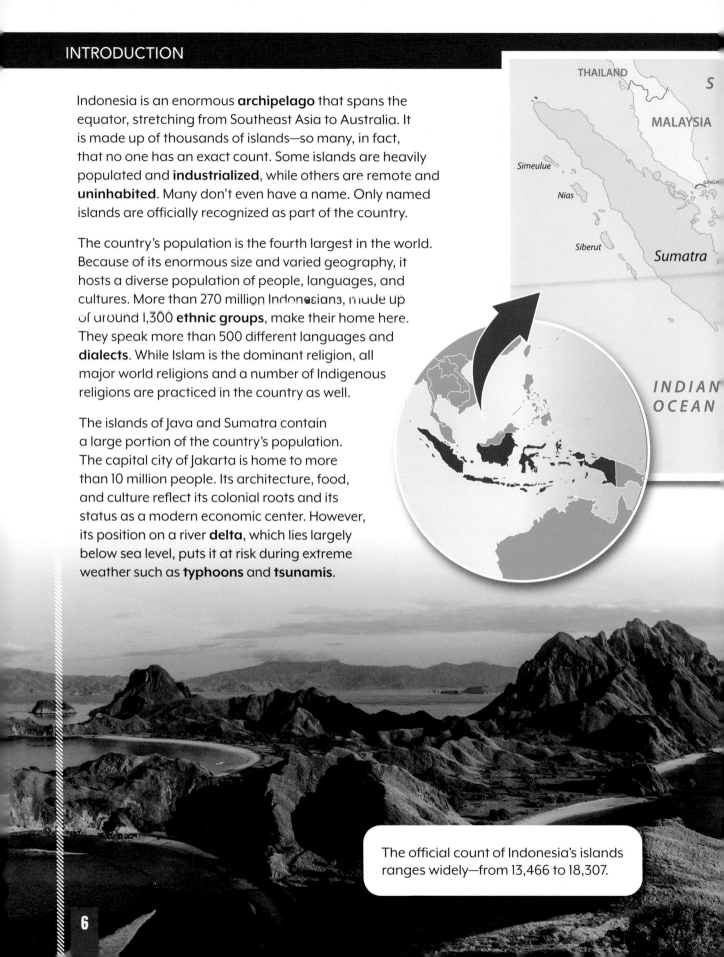

THAILAND

S

MALAYSIA

Simeulue

SINGA

Nias

Siberut

Sumatra

INDIAN
OCEAN

The official count of Indonesia's islands ranges widely—from 13,466 to 18,307.

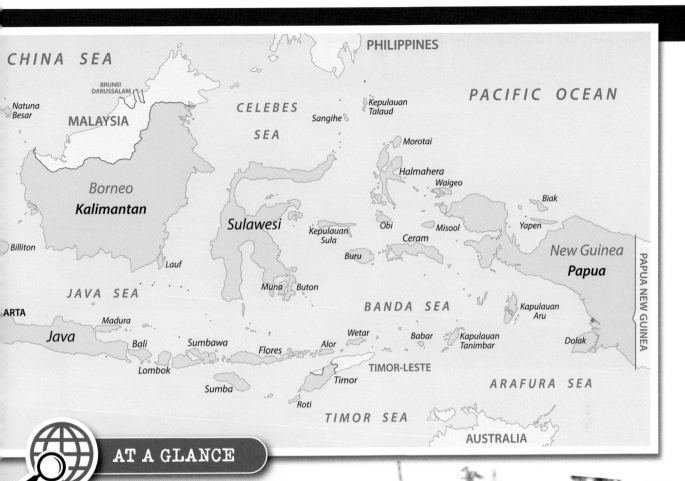

CHINA SEA

PHILIPPINES

BRUNEI DARUSSALAM

Natuna Besar

MALAYSIA

CELEBES

SEA

Kepulauan Talaud

PACIFIC OCEAN

Sangihe

Morotai

Borneo
Kalimantan

Halmahera
Waigeo

Biak

Billiton

Sulawesi

Kepulauan Sula

Obi

Ceram

Misool

Yapen

New Guinea
Papua

Lauf

Buru

Muna Buton

BANDA SEA

Kapulauan Aru

PAPUA NEW GUINEA

JAVA SEA

ARTA

Madura

Java

Bali

Sumbawa

Flores

Alor

Wetar

Babar

Kapulauan Tanimbar

Dolak

Lombok

TIMOR-LESTE

ARAFURA SEA

Sumba

Timor

Roti

TIMOR SEA

AUSTRALIA

AT A GLANCE

- **OFFICIAL NAME:**
  Republic of Indonesia

- **NATIONAL CAPITAL:** Jakarta

- **POPULATION:** 275,400,000

- **OFFICIAL LANGUAGE:**
  Indonesian (*Bahasa Indonesia*)

- **LAND AREA:** 740,122 square miles
  (1,916,907 sq. km)

Almost half of Indonesia's population lives in rural areas. The rest are urban dwellers.

The Land

The major Indonesian islands have forested volcanic mountains in their interiors. These slope downward to **plains** along their coasts.

Indonesia covers a territory that stretches 3,200 miles (5,100 km) from east to west and 1,100 miles (1,800 km) from north to south. It is bordered by the Indian Ocean to the west and the Pacific Ocean to the east. The five main islands are Java, Sumatra, Kalimantan, Sulawesi, and Papua. They make up most of Indonesia's land mass and population. Three islands—Borneo, Timor, and Papua—share territory with other countries. Java, one of the largest islands, contains the country's most **fertile** agricultural land.

Because it covers such a wide geographic area, Indonesia's landscapes are incredibly rich and diverse—from lush rain forests to coastal mangrove swamps and rich coral reefs. Its mountain ranges rise up to 12,450 feet (3,800 m) above sea level on several islands, including Sumatra, Java, Bali, and Lombok. In total, Indonesia boasts a whopping 61,500 miles (99,000 km) of coastline, with long, sandy beaches and the world's largest coral reef system. But this same coastline makes the country extremely **vulnerable** to tsunamis, monsoon flooding, and rising ocean levels.

Monsoons are changes in wind patterns that bring wet and dry seasons.

Volcanic Activity

Indonesia's massive coastline is not the only factor that makes the country vulnerable to natural disasters. Its many active volcanoes are also a concern. Indonesia is located between two of the world's most active volcanic belts: the Ring of Fire and the Alpide Belt. These belts are made up of a series of volcanoes that run along the bottom of the Pacific Ocean. The volcanoes frequently erupt, causing earthquakes and tsunamis. Of the country's 400 volcanoes, more than 100 are active, meaning they are capable of erupting at some point in the future. Some of the world's most violent eruptions have occurred in Indonesia. In December 2022, thousands of people were evacuated from their villages on the island of Java when Mount Semeru erupted.

In 1815, Mount Tambora on the island of Sumbawa discharged such enormous amounts of ash into Earth's atmosphere that it clouded the Sun. It was the largest recorded eruption in human history.

Indonesia is one of many countries around the world that use the Volcano Disaster Assistance Program (VDAP) to help monitor volcanoes and respond to crises.

The 24,000-mile-long (40,000 km) horseshoe-shaped Ring of Fire is the site of most of the world's earthquakes and around 75 percent of the world's volcanoes.

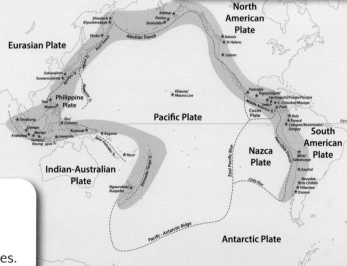

Climate and Weather

Indonesia's location near the equator means that its climate is mostly tropical. Weather is typically hot, humid, and rainy. Warm ocean waters balance the land temperatures so that there is little change in temperature between seasons and day and night. Only in the higher mountain elevations do the temperatures drop off enough to make evenings cool and occasionally chilly.

Unlike many other countries, Indonesia does not have four weather seasons. Only two—rainy or dry—make up its seasons. Although slight variations occur across this huge archipelago, the dry season generally takes place from April to October. The rainy season occurs from November to March. As **climate change** has intensified, however, these seasons have become a little less predictable. Climate change poses a significant challenge in Indonesia because its immense coastline is vulnerable to rising sea levels due to warming oceans.

Millions of people live in Indonesia's low-lying coastal areas. Their communities and livelihoods are threatened by rising sea levels.

Jakarta has an average high temperature of around 86 degrees Fahrenheit (30 °C).

The island of Borneo receives around 10 inches (25 cm) of rain per month.

Wind and rain play important roles in shaping Indonesia's climate. Monsoon winds blowing from different directions influence rainy and dry seasons. During the dry season, warm winds move northwest from Australia's deserts, toward the equator. In the wet season, an opposite system occurs as wind moves down from Asia. This wind combines with humid winds from the Indian Ocean, causing large amounts of rainfall.

Other wind patterns and island **topographies** cause climate differences across the archipelago. The southwest coast of the island of Sumatra is incredibly rainy. It can get up to 120 to 155 inches (300 to 390 cm) of rain during a year. The extremely wet and humid conditions provide an ideal climate for lush, dense rain forests. Due to Jakarta's location on Java's northwest coast, it has a longer rainy season, from October to May. This is followed by a short dry season, from June to September.

High winds and rains during rainy season threaten many coastal communities.

Teak

Plants and Wildlife

More than 3,000 species of trees can be found across Indonesia. Many of them are harvested for economic purposes. Oil from the sandalwood tree is used to make perfume, soap, incense, and medicine. The tree is also prized for its **aromatic** wood. Rattan vines, which grow in Indonesia's rain forests, are used for furniture. Teak wood, also popular in furniture, is one of Java's largest **exports**. Rasamala, an evergreen that thrives in Indonesia's tropical climate, is harvested for its timber. It is also used in local medicines and to make incense.

Mangrove forests grow in the muddy shores along many of Indonesia's islands. They provide Indonesia's coastlines with valuable protection from devastating monsoons and tsunamis. The tree roots minimize land **erosion** and the trees themselves act as a barrier to stop tall waves and help prevent flooding. Mangrove forests are also important habitats for many fish. Efforts are being made to restore forests that have been lost after being cleared for agriculture and fish farming.

Sandalwood

Rasamala

The giant Komodo dragon can grow up to 12 feet (3.7 m) long.

Rehabilitation programs have been established to help save the endangered Sumatran orangutan, which is **native** to Sumatra.

The island of Java lost 70 percent of its coastal mangroves due to **deforestation**. This has caused significant loss of coastal land and threatens the survival of people who live there.

Indonesia's waters are home to an incredible variety of fish species. Many are harvested for food and exported around the world. In fact, Indonesia is the second-largest fish producer in the world. Some of its most important exports are shrimp, squid, lobster, crab, and tuna. Other species, such as tetras, corys, and clown fish, are bred for aquariums.

Indonesia straddles the boundary between Asian and Australian wildlife habitats. This means it has an incredibly diverse range of animals from each continent. To its west, closer to Asia, are populations of rhinoceroses, orangutans, tigers, and elephants. The eastern islands are habitats for cockatoos, birds of paradise, and bandicoots—animals closely related to those found in Australia. Many islands host species found nowhere else, such as the Komodo dragon, which lives on the Sunda Islands. Javan rhinoceroses have become extremely endangered and can now only be found in Java's Ujung Kulon National Park.

Settlement in Indonesia

Positioned at the crossroads of the Pacific and Indian Oceans, Indonesia historically attracted settlers and traders traveling by sea. Today, it is home to more than 270 million people, spread across hundreds of islands.

More than half of Indonesia's population lives on the island of Java. This is the result of a thriving agricultural economy that has been practiced there for more than 4,000 years. From as early as the 1st century, it attracted traders from Asia in search of valuable spices. Later, traders from Europe arrived. In the 16th century, Indonesia became the heart of the Dutch **colonial empire**.

Subsistence farmers grow only enough food to support themselves and their families.

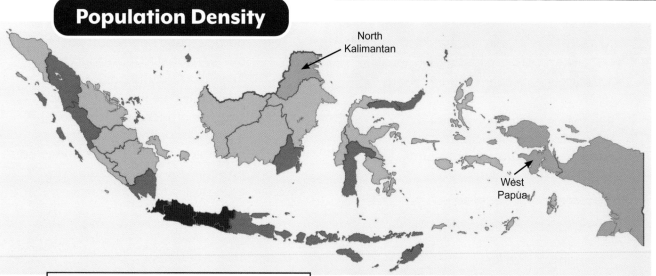

Population Density

North Kalimantan

West Papua

Provinces of Indonesia by population density in 2020 (per square kilometer)
(1 square kilometer = 0.39 square miles)

- ■ 10,001 and above
- ■ 1,001 to 10,000
- ■ 101 to 1,000
- ■ 11 to 100
- ■ 1 to 10

North Kalimantan and West Papua have the smallest populations—other than the many islands that are completely uninhabited. They are inhabited by local Indigenous peoples who live in rural agricultural and small fishing communities.

Agricultural and Coastal Settlement

Java's fertile agricultural land is largely used for growing rice. But corn, cassavas, peanuts, soybeans, tobacco, coffee, tea, rubber, and sugarcane are also important crops. Much of Java's large population remains rural. Sumatra is Indonesia's second most populous island. Arab and Indian traders arrived there in the 6th and 7th centuries. Its fertile agricultural lands have been largely dedicated to growing coffee, which has become highly prized around the world.

The rich volcanic soils and tropical climate of Indonesia's highland regions support many groups of people who have made their living raising cattle, growing rice, and practicing subsistence farming. The country's extensive coastline and abundance of fish have supported Indigenous coastal communities for thousands of years. As shipping routes between Indonesia, Asia, and Europe were established, some coastal communities became the site of **port** cities. From these ports, the country's crops and natural resources were shipped to markets overseas.

Jakarta's port is the largest in Indonesia. Millions of tons of **cargo** pass through it each year. More than 18,000 people are employed there.

Becoming Indonesia

Ancient Kingdoms to Colonization

Indonesia's natural resources, strategic position along trade routes, and location between Asia and Australia have played major roles in shaping human settlement over many centuries. Ancient land bridges, which once connected Indonesia with Southeast Asia, allowed the first human migration to the region thousands of years ago. Archaeological sites suggest humans settled there at least 100,000 years ago. Early Indigenous communities grew crops, hunted, and fished.

The first Buddhists and Hindus arrived from India around 100 to 200 C.E. They traveled to Indonesia using a **maritime** trade route between India and Indonesia. These settlers included traders, sailors, and religious scholars. Some of their first settlements were on the islands of Java and Sumatra. By the 1400s, several Buddhist and Hindu kingdoms ruled over large parts of Indonesia.

The bustling cultural center of Yogyakarta, on the island of Java, began as an early settlement around 732 C.E.

Hindu temples around Indonesia reflect the country's early history.

The Maluku Islands, or the Moluccas, are located in eastern Indonesia.

Islamic traders arrived from India and **Persia** in the 1200s. They first settled in coastal areas, then spread farther inland. They introduced Islam to the country, which grew to become the dominant religion. The Portuguese arrived in 1512. They were eager to **exploit** the region's rich spices, which were highly prized back in Europe. The Maluku Islands held spice resources that could not be found elsewhere. For this reason, they became known as the Spice Islands.

The Dutch came in 1599 and quickly seized control of the spice trade from the Portuguese. They established the Dutch East India Company and started an aggressive campaign to colonize the islands. They seized control of lands and **enslaved** people to farm crops to be exported back to Europe. Regional outposts and ports were created to control the export and trade of coffee, spices, and sugar.

To grow its empire, the Dutch imported hundreds of thousands of **plantation** workers from places such as China and India. These laborers were treated harshly and bound by contracts to work with no pay.

Terraced fields are perfect for growing rice. The crop needs to be irrigated often, so the terraces help slow the flow of water away from the fields. They also help decrease land erosion.

In the Middle Ages, nutmeg was the rarest spice in the world— worth its weight in gold.

Expanding Agriculture

Rice is a main part of the diet of Indonesian people. It has been the foundation of Indonesia's agricultural heritage for thousands of years. It was traditionally grown on small-scale farms and harvested by individual families. Today, lush rice terraces occupy much of the agricultural land on the islands of Java, Sumatra, and Sulawesi. But Indonesia's tropical climate and fertile volcanic soils make it an ideal place to grow other agricultural crops as well. These have played an enormous role in the settlement of Indonesia and the expansion of its agricultural economy.

The Maluku Islands, or Spice Islands, were renowned for the incredible variety of spices that grew there: cloves, cinnamon, nutmeg, pepper, and mace. The unique flavors and healing properties of spices were highly prized in Europe and Asia. Arab traders first arrived in the Maluku Islands to trade silk, coffee, and ivory for spices. Eventually, Portuguese and Dutch colonizers followed, eager to control the trade of these valuable crops.

Planting New Cash Crops

As the Dutch expanded their colony across Indonesia, they discovered that the region was well-suited to growing lucrative crops. They introduced coffee in the 17th century, bringing seedlings from Yemen. The first coffee plantations were established around Batavia, or present-day Jakarta. They were then expanded across Java to Sumatra and Sulawesi. Roads and railways were built to transport the harvests from the islands' interiors to coastal ports, which were developed as hubs to export these goods overseas.

Sugar was also introduced to Java. Flat lands along rivers were ideal for the large-scale plantations they established. Factories were built to process the raw sugarcane before it could be exported. Many of these factories were the basis for the expanding **infrastructure** that drove Indonesia's development in the 1800s.

Today, many companies use trucks to transport crops because of lower costs and improvements to road infrastructure.

Indonesia is a top exporter of agricultural products.

The Dutch ordered Indonesian farmers to grow crops that would be most valuable for the colony, such as sugar, coffee (right), and tea.

Exploiting Natural Resources

As rapid industrialization took place across Europe in the 1800s, the demand for natural resources was unstoppable. The Dutch East India Company continued to exploit Indonesia's resources to meet the demand for new products. They introduced rubber plantations to the islands of Sumatra and Kalimantan. Until then, these islands had been **sparsely** populated by people who grew rice for food. Rubber grew well in Indonesia's tropical climate and was in high demand in Europe as modern machinery was developed. But its introduction in Indonesia brought enormous and devastating changes to the landscape. Large areas of jungle were cleared to make way for the plantations. Suddenly, local farmers found themselves competing with large Dutch plantations for land.

Estimates say that anywhere from 40 to 80 percent of logging in Indonesia is illegal, putting the country's forests at risk. Environmentalists are calling on the government to do more, such as enforcing laws, to end the practice.

Teak wood grew abundantly in Indonesia's dense rain forests. The wood is strong and water-resistant, making it ideal for use in construction. Ancient Hindus and Buddhists used it to build temples. The Dutch needed it for their ships, but also for the bridges, homes, and warehouses they were building as they expanded their empire. Java was the center of the teak industry in Indonesia. Over the years that followed, global demand for teak has severely threatened Indonesia's old-growth forests.

Indigenous people lived on the islands of Bangka and Belitung, east of Sumatra, for centuries, surviving off the bountiful fishing grounds along their coasts. But the Dutch began mining tin there in the 19th century to meet demand for the mineral in manufacturing processes. Mining soon changed the landscape of these remote, pristine islands. Indonesia is still one of the world's top producers of tin. Mining tin is a huge part of the economy in Bangka and Belitung today.

Many of Indonesia's modern cities—such as Makassar (top) and Palembang (middle)—were established along ancient trade routes. They became important hubs for the storage and export of agricultural goods, and as bases for colonial expansion.

Tin mining has damaged the coral reefs and mangrove forests around the Bangka and Belitung islands.

Indonesia Today

Indonesia's Ethnic Groups

Modern Indonesia is a country of incredibly rich ethnic diversity. Centuries of human migration, trade, and colonization have shaped human settlement in Indonesia. There are more than 1,000 ethnic groups who call Indonesia home. But it is difficult, if not impossible, to define them in simple terms. Indonesian ethnic groups can be used to define a people's location, language, religion, or culture. Three of the main ethnic groups in Indonesia are the Javanese, the Sundanese, and the Batak people.

The Javanese people represent about 40 percent of the country's population—roughly 100 million people. Most live in the densely populated industrial and agricultural regions of central and eastern Java. The principal Javanese cities are Yogyakarta, Surakarta, and Jakarta. The artistic and religious cultures of the Javanese people have been shaped by the ancient Hindu and Buddhist kingdoms that once ruled there. Their legacy lives on in Borobudur, which is one of the world's most impressive Buddhist temples. The language spoken is Javanese.

The massive Borobudur temple was discovered in 1815 after being covered in volcanic ash for years.

Farming is a big part of life for many Javanese people.

About 40 million people identify as Sundanese. They are an agriculture-based people, located on western Java, who make their living mostly from rice crops. It is believed they originally migrated there from Southeast Asia and Oceania. Their capital city, Bandung, is known for its Dutch architecture, as it was a key city for the Dutch colonists who established plantations nearby. The Sundanese people speak Sundanese.

Sundanese and Javanese culture is similar. One key difference is language. Another is the more communal lifestyle of the Sundanese.

The Batak people of North Sumatra are thought to have **originated** from a tribal people who migrated from Southeast Asia. They number about 8.5 million and are one of the largest Indigenous groups in Indonesia. They speak Batak as their main language and are known for their intricate art. They make their living through agriculture, fishing, and hunting.

Tor-tor dance, traditionally performed by the Batak people during funerals and other ceremonies, is one of the oldest dances in Indonesia.

23

21st-Century Economy

As Indonesia moved from an agricultural economy to an industrial one, its population shifted from rural to urban. Java is the economic heart of the country and the most heavily populated area, accounting for half of the country's total population.

Agriculture, however, remains an important part of Indonesia's economy. The country is an important global producer of agricultural products such as rice, palm oil, cinnamon, cloves, coffee, and cocoa. Agriculture is based on the islands of Java and Sumatra. Although teak continues to be harvested in Java, plywood and **wood veneers** have become an important export product for Kalimantan. Indonesia is the world's second-largest rubber producer, with large plantations on Sumatra, Riau, Jambi, and West Kalimantan.

Rubber is made from latex, a liquid substance found within rubber trees (above). After the latex is collected, it is processed to **extract** the rubber, which is rolled out and dried (below).

Around half of farmers in Indonesia are smallholders. They have smaller farms of less than 5 acres (2 hectares). These farms are often independent, family-run operations.

In the 1990s, manufacturing became the largest sector of Indonesia's economy as the government supported a shift toward industrialization.

Around 10 percent of Indonesian workers are employed in the tourism industry.

Indonesia's mining industry continues to revolve around tin mining. The country is the world's second-largest exporter of this metal, with 90 percent of its production from the islands of Bangka and Belitung. Today, tin is in demand as an important component in the production of electronic goods.

With its long coastline and abundant fish species, it is not surprising that Indonesia is one of the world's largest fish producers. Industrial farms on western Java and southern Sumatra raise shrimp and milkfish for export around the world. Deep-sea harvests take advantage of Indonesia's ocean stocks of tuna, snapper, and mackerel.

Tourism grew dramatically in the 20th century as Indonesia became known for its spectacular beaches, lush mountain rain forests, and rich cultural heritage. The island of Bali, with its white-sand beaches, is the country's primary tourist attraction. But tourists also are attracted by the country's exotic wildlife and ancient civilizations.

Life in Indonesia

After centuries of colonization, Indonesians finally achieved their independence in 1945. Since then, a rapidly growing population and manufacturing industry have transformed the country into a modern economic power. Its economy is now firmly positioned among the top 20 in the world.

Government-funded programs have lifted millions of Indonesians out of poverty. The country has a rapidly growing middle class. But 1 in 10 Indonesians still live in poverty. Urban populations tend to have higher standards of living than rural communities.

In a country made up of thousands of islands, providing adequate infrastructure for the entire population has been one of the biggest challenges. Infrastructure includes the systems and services that help a society operate, such as roads and power plants. Many communities on remote islands have limited or no access to Internet, safe food and water, health care, and education. There is also a need for reliable power and transportation systems for goods and people. Improving infrastructure is a key goal for government.

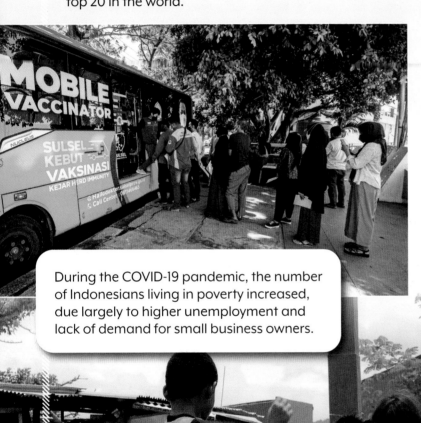

During the COVID-19 pandemic, the number of Indonesians living in poverty increased, due largely to higher unemployment and lack of demand for small business owners.

Indonesia's infrastructure challenges are more pronounced during extreme weather events, making communities more vulnerable to damage.

The Fight for Independence

A movement seeking Indonesian independence grew rapidly in the 20th century. Many Indonesians were dissatisfied with the structure of authority that the Dutch had established and wanted more power to determine their future. Their goal was to create a modern country that embraced the ethnic diversity of its citizens. But many local rulers, called rajas, resisted the movement. They had built their wealth by supporting the Dutch.

Sukarno was the leader of the independence movement and became Indonesia's first president in 1949.

The nationalist movement proclaimed Indonesia's independence on August 17, 1945. This started the Indonesian National Revolution. More than 100,000 Indonesians would die over four years of conflict with Dutch forces and other military groups before the country was granted full independence in 1949. In the years that followed, there were shortages of food, fuel, and clothing. New systems of government, **currency**, and laws had to be established. But the Indonesian people were hungry for change and were determined to move forward with their new nation.

The Indonesian National Revolution not only ended colonial rule, but also the rule of the rajas.

Independence Day is a national holiday in Indonesia, celebrated on August 17 each year.

Human Impact on Environment

Generations of Indigenous peoples have traditionally served as guardians of Indonesia's natural environment. Rural Indonesians have long practiced traditions of living **sustainably** off the land and seas—from rice-growing farmers on the terraces of Bali's hillsides to subsistence farmers in highland communities and coastal fishing communities in Sulawesi.

However, as Indonesia rushed to modernize, its natural environments have been put under increasing pressure. **Mechanization**, the use of chemical fertilizers, and the increasing intensity of crop production have changed agricultural practices and threatened soil health. Coastal fishers have seen their catches devastated by overfishing, **aquaculture** farms, and the destruction of local fish habitats. Highland farmers have also been crowded out by industrial logging operations.

Fishing is an important source of food and livelihood for many Indonesians.

Close to 200 ships pass through the Strait of Malacca each day.

More than 30 million Indonesians depend on the country's rain forests to earn a living. During the last century, mining and plantation crops have destroyed large areas of rain forest and devastated Indigenous communities. Forest fires and **commercial** logging in places such as Kalimantan and Sumatra also furthered the rate of deforestation and soil erosion. Native species, including the Sumatran tiger, are on the brink of extinction as their habitats are destroyed. The country lost more than 69 million acres (28 million hectares) of forest between 2001 and 2021. However, recent policies to protect forests, such as forest fire mitigation, have slowed the rate of deforestation.

Indonesia also has some of the worst water pollution in Asia. Some of the main reasons for this are inadequate sewer systems in major cities, large-scale industrial waste that is poorly treated, and fertilizer runoff from agriculture. The heavily traveled shipping routes through the Strait of Malacca regularly experience oil leaks from tanker ships. Mercury used in mining extraction also contaminates water sources, endangering fish and local communities.

Trees take in carbon dioxide, a **greenhouse gas**. Because of this, deforestation is a big reason Indonesia is a major global emitter of greenhouse gases.

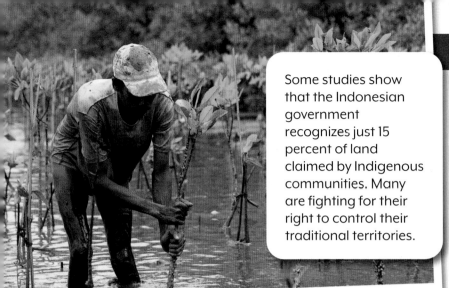

Some studies show that the Indonesian government recognizes just 15 percent of land claimed by Indigenous communities. Many are fighting for their right to control their traditional territories.

Environmental Protections

Indonesia is continuing to expand its economy through the extraction of its natural resources. As it does so, it will need to find ways to balance these activities while honoring and restoring rural Indigenous guardianship of traditional lands.

Since 1960, the government has tried to **enact** stronger environmental laws and develop programs to help manage the country's natural resources. But they have achieved only limited success because many of the laws are poorly enforced or too easily ignored by powerful industry leaders and organizations. The palm oil industry is one of the biggest environmental offenders.

The Indonesian government has committed to restoring nearly 1.5 million acres (600,000 hectares) of mangrove forests by 2024. Some environmentalists, however, believe that conserving existing mangroves would be a more effective use of money and effort.

Government regulations have tried to make fishing more sustainable by controlling where fishing can occur and supporting fishers in using equipment and practices that do not damage ecosystems.

Closer Look

Palm Oil Production

The Dutch introduced oil palm trees to Indonesia in the late 19th century. Since then, the palm oil industry has exploded. Today, Indonesia is the world's leading producer of palm oil. But palm oil production has had enormous environmental consequences. Huge areas of rain forest and farmland across Sumatra, Borneo, and Kalimantan have been destroyed to make way for large-scale plantations. A number of laws enacted in 1999 required companies seeking **permits** for new plantations to consult with local Indigenous communities to assess the risks of

Indigenous communities in Indonesia depend on the rain forests to survive.

further development. But in most cases, this has not happened. The Indonesia Sustainable Palm Oil (ISPO) standard was established in 2009, but it is poorly enforced. In 2018, the Indonesian president announced a moratorium, or temporary ban, on new permits for palm oil plantations. This was one factor that has helped slow the rate of deforestation in recent years. But its expiry in 2021 means further deforestation is almost certain. Indigenous communities in these regions continue to see their way of life destroyed as their land is taken from them illegally.

Palm oil is used in many goods and products, from food and cosmetics to biofuels.

A Vibrant Country

A Multicultural Society

Indonesia's complex geography and its diverse blend of ethnicities have paved the way for a unique mix of languages and religions. Most Indonesians speak the language of their ethnic group, such as Javanese, Malay, Batak, or Balinese, as their first language at home with family and friends.

The country's official language is Indonesian, a form of the Malay language that was commonly spoken during the period of the colonial Dutch East Indies. It was introduced in order to help unify the country through a common language and to support the economy of the newly independent country. As such, it became a strong symbol of national unity. It is used across the country's education, business, political, and media sectors. With the exception of only the most remote communities, it is widely understood across the country. English, however, is also widely used in major cities and regional tourist destinations, and is the language of international business.

The Indonesian **constitution mandates** that Indonesian is the language used in schools—sometimes posing challenges for the estimated 90 percent of students who have a different first language.

Animism is deeply rooted in Indonesia. Its origins go back to ancient Javanese society, in which people believed that all living things have souls.

Religion

Modern Indonesia's constitution guarantees its citizens the freedom to worship according to their own personal beliefs. Buddhism and Hinduism, which were brought to Indonesia by ancient traders, are still practiced today in some places around the country. So, too, is Christianity—introduced by the Dutch as they colonized the country. But Islam is Indonesia's main religion, with almost 9 out of 10 people practicing it. Five official religions are recognized by the country's constitution: Islam, Christianity, Hinduism, Buddhism, and **Confucianism**. They reflect the diversity of the people who have traded and settled in the country. While it is not recognized officially as a religion, several ethnic groups continue to practice animism, a form of worship of the natural environment.

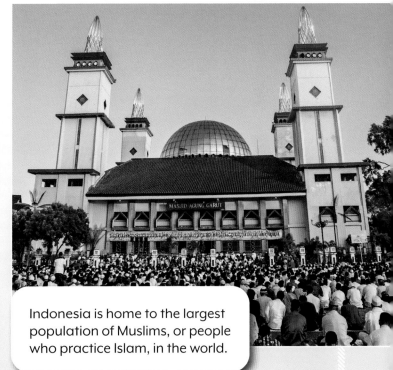

Indonesia is home to the largest population of Muslims, or people who practice Islam, in the world.

Festivals and Celebrations

Many of Indonesia's holidays reflect the different religions practiced there. Muslims celebrate Hari Raya Idul Fitri to mark the end of Ramadan, the month of fasting, prayer, and reflection. Nyepi, or "Day of Silence," is celebrated by Hindus to bring in the New Year. Indonesia's Buddhists celebrate Hari Waisak to commemorate the birth and **enlightenment** of Buddha. On August 17, the entire country celebrates Hari Proklamasi, Indonesia's Independence Day. This event commemorates the date when Indonesians proclaimed their independence from their Dutch colonial rulers. Flag-raising ceremonies, parades, competitions, and celebrations take place across the country.

Some of Indonesia's festivals have rather unusual stories. Yadnya Kasada is celebrated by the Tenggerese people of eastern Java. The people make a pilgrimage up Mount Bromo, an active volcano rising 7,641 feet (2,329 m). There, they throw offerings, such as food, livestock, and money, into the volcano. This tradition came from a legend that tells the story of a couple who begged the mountain gods to help them have a child. The gods granted them 24 children—on the condition that a 25th child had to be thrown into the volcano as a sacrifice. The Tenggerese believe that continuing to throw sacrifices, or offerings, into the volcano **appeases** the gods.

Nyepi is mostly celebrated in Bali, where restrictions are placed on daily activities to encourage a day of self-reflection only. These include no light, including electricity, no working, and no traveling.

After catching the sea worms during the festival, Lombok locals may cook them, add them to dishes such as soup, or eat them raw.

Hari Raya Indul Fitri is also known in Indonesia as Lebaran, and in other parts of the world as Eid al-Fitr. It is celebrated around the world with gatherings, gifts, and prayer.

The Sasak people celebrate Bau Nyale— the Catching the Sea Worms Festival—on the island of Lombok each February when the sea worms surface. The Sasak believe that the sea worms are sacred—capable of bringing people either prosperity or hardship. This belief is based on an ancient legend about a princess who tried to drown herself at sea. When villagers went into the water to rescue her, they found only sea worms in her place. The Sasak believe that the sea worms are the **reincarnated** princess. The festival is celebrated with competitions, rowing demonstrations, and art performances that reenact the princess's story.

Wayang kulit

A Rich Cultural Heritage

A rich culture of music, theater, and dance has its origins in Indonesia's ancient practices, religions, and Indigenous beliefs. Wayang is a style of theater performed with leather or wooden puppets. It originated on the island of Java, introduced by the ancient Buddhists and Hindus who came to Indonesia. Many wayang stories are based on legendary Hindu tales of the struggle between good and evil. Wayang kulit—or shadow puppet theater—is the most popular form. It features puppet silhouettes, which are projected onto a screen to tell a story. Wayang is traditionally performed at sacred temple ceremonies or in village celebrations.

Wayang performances can last many, many hours.

Gamelan percussion instruments are often made of metal. This material does not break down or grow mold in Indonesia's humid climate.

Gamelan music is made by an ensemble of percussion and other instruments, such as xylophones, drums, large metal gongs, and, sometimes, bamboo flutes and stringed instruments. Its name comes from the Javanese word *gamel*, which means "to strike or hammer." It is believed to date back to an ancient Indigenous culture. Legend suggests that the god who ruled Java needed a way to summon the other gods and so he invented the gong. When he added other instruments, the gamelan ensemble was created. Gamelan music is often used to accompany dance performances, puppet theater, and religious ceremonies.

Hundreds of traditional dance styles can be found across Indonesia. Some have their origins in the ceremonial court dances of Java's royal palaces. Others reflect the

In the *Kipas Pakarena* dance, dancers wave colorful fans—or *kipas*—in elaborate movements to tell the legend of the departure of ancient gods from Earth to heaven. It is believed that before they left, these gods taught humans how to hunt and farm.

traditions and beliefs of Indonesia's many Indigenous groups. Topeng—or mask—dances were first performed in the ancient Hindu-Buddhist royal courts. They feature elaborate masks in white, gold, or red to tell the stories of legendary kings, heroes, and mythology.

Textiles, Weaving, and Batik

Songket

Blangkon

Clothing and handicrafts in Indonesia pay tribute to its environment, natural resources, cultures, and traditions. Traditional Balinese clothing is heavily influenced by the styles of the ancient Hindu royal court. It is often colorful and intricate. Traditional clothing in Jakarta is influenced by the Indian, Arabic, Chinese, and Malaysian people who settled there. The blangkon—a traditional batik headdress worn by Javanese men—originates from the turbans worn by ancient Indian traders. The sarong—a long piece of fabric that is wrapped into a skirt and worn by both men and women—was introduced by the Malay people. The kebaya is a blouse made of silk, cotton, or lace. Once worn by women in the royal court, it was adopted by the Dutch before becoming part of everyday clothing for Indonesian women.

Tenun Ikat

Weaving is practiced in a variety of regions. Its designs, colors, and fabrics are inspired by local cultures, **textiles**, and dyes. *Songket*, from South Sumatra, is woven from silk or cotton and uses gold or silver thread to create delicate patterns. Many are symbolic of the natural environment. *Tenun Ikat,* from East Nusa Tenggara province, uses local plants, leaves, and roots to create natural dyes.

Kebaya

Payas Agung is traditional Balinese clothing known for its intricacy and luxury. It is usually worn for weddings.

Batik

Batik is the art of creating elaborate designs on fabric using a wooden block printing technique. It was introduced to Indonesia in the 17th century by Asian traders who bought and sold textiles on the island of Java. Over time, textile merchants perfected the technique. They used local raw materials including cotton, beeswax, and natural dyes made from local plants. Batik techniques and designs are wide-ranging and have different meanings. Patterns, materials, and colors reflect the natural resources available from one region to another. Batik cloth from Java is exported around the world. It is an important industry and a unique piece of Indonesian culture.

Batik artists create intricate designs using tools such as stamps, pen-like cantings, and brushes.

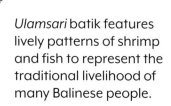

Ulamsari batik features lively patterns of shrimp and fish to represent the traditional livelihood of many Balinese people.

The *Sekar Jagad* pattern—which means "map of the world"—represents Indonesia's rich diversity.

Looking to the Future

Balancing Future Goals

As it looks to the future, a challenge for Indonesia will be to balance economic goals with protections for the environment and Indigenous rights. Indonesia's goal is to become a major economic force in the global economy. In 2020, the government passed a package of laws to help create jobs and grow the economy. But environmentalists worry these laws will actually weaken environmental protections. They may also restrict the rights of Indigenous communities to review projects that impact their lands.

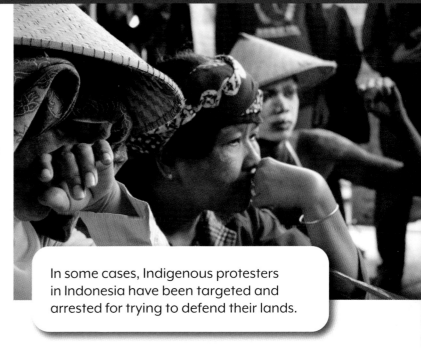

In some cases, Indigenous protesters in Indonesia have been targeted and arrested for trying to defend their lands.

More than 50 million Indigenous peoples live in Indonesia. Although Indonesia adopted the United Nations Declaration on the Rights of Indigenous Peoples, it has never fully supported its Indigenous population's land and human rights claims. Incidents of violence and discrimination have increased, particularly in places where projects pursue Indigenous territory for development.

Tin mining, a huge industry in Indonesia, can have serious consequences for delicate coastal environments. On the Bangka and Belitung islands, local fishers are fighting against a government plan to allow tin mining along the coast.

AMAN

In order to address issues of discrimination and marginalization of Indigenous peoples in Indonesia, a group called AMAN was created. It stands for *Aliansi Masyarakat Adat Nusantara*, or the Indigenous Peoples Alliance of the Archipelago. AMAN represents more than 15 million people from 2,230 Indigenous communities across Indonesia. The group's goal is to empower Indonesia's Indigenous peoples to protect their lands, their culture, and the natural environment for future generations. They hope to do this in several ways. They want Indigenous peoples to gain ownership over their ancestral lands in order to protect them. They would like to be consulted and asked for consent on any development projects that involve their lands. A "zero violence" principle would ensure that community leaders are not **criminalized** for defending their lands. Funding for education, health care, and rural development would help encourage sustainable development.

Using ancestral Indigenous knowledge of the land in Indonesia could help prevent and address climate change. One way is by practicing more sustainable agriculture methods.

AMAN points out that Indigenous knowledge and practices can help Indonesia mitigate the impact of natural disasters. One example is earthquake-resistant housing built by the Sasak people.

The 2007 UN Declaration on the Rights of Indigenous Peoples was a resolution that affirmed Indigenous peoples' right to land, freedom, self-government, culture, and more.

The Paris Climate Agreement is an international treaty signed by 196 countries. Each pledged to limit greenhouse gas emissions in order to curb global warming.

Environmental Challenges

Increasing population density, rapid **urbanization**, and the industrialization of farming, fishing, and forestry have strained the country's natural environment and its resources. The government will have to find ways to balance the demands of a growing population that needs housing, jobs, and food with strategies to protect the environment.

Globally, Indonesia is considered a serious environmental offender. It is the largest coal exporter in the world and one of the biggest sources of carbon emissions, which cause global warming. It has also faced heavy criticism for the widespread destruction of its rain forests. The world is beginning to demand that nations find more sustainable ways to grow their economies. Indonesia will need creative solutions if it is to meet its commitments to the Paris Climate Agreement, signed in 2015. The government says it is committed to transitioning to become a greener economy.

Sustainable teak plantations and regulations were established in the 20th century to protect Java's old-growth teak forests from widespread deforestation.

Greener Solutions

A project in Kalimantan aims to create the world's largest green **industrial park**. It hopes to attract manufacturers of green technology such as solar panels and electric-car batteries. It also plans to reduce carbon emissions by developing more environmentally friendly manufacturing processes to produce "greener" aluminum.

On the island of Batam, a huge solar project is planned. When it is completed, it will be the largest of its kind in the world, allowing Indonesia to create new renewable energy sources. The energy created there could supply islands across Indonesia and even other countries in Southeast Asia.

The government claims it is committed to phasing out coal production. It plans to discontinue approval for any new coal-

TransJakarta, a public transportation system in Jakarta, has started a project to convert 3,000 diesel-powered buses to electric. It plans to have 10,000 electric buses by 2030.

powered factories. But environmental experts say the government must go further. They want construction that is already underway for new plants to be stopped. They also want plants that are in production to be closed.

Coal mines provide jobs for around 250,000 people in Indonesia. Finding jobs for these workers is one challenge related to ending coal operations.

The Threat of Climate Change

Climate change poses real threats to countries around the world. But it will be especially devastating for island nations. As sea levels rise, many of Indonesia's islands could become unlivable or could disappear completely.

The definition of an island means it cannot be covered by water at high tide. Experts predict this could mean more than 1,500 of Indonesia's islands could disappear by 2050 as a result of rising oceans. Indonesia's official island count ranges between 13,466 and 18,307. An exact count has never been formalized. As Indonesia loses islands to climate change, it will have less authority over regional trade routes, shipping lanes, and territorial fishing rights. This will have dramatic consequences for its economy and people. Some estimates suggest that 110 million Indonesians—including many in coastal communities and the urban poor—have already been affected by climate change.

In coastal cities with high population densities, many urban Indonesians live in poverty in **informal settlements** along riverbanks and in flood zones. They are especially vulnerable to the effects of climate change.

Indonesia's extensive coral reefs and fishing industry could be devastated by climate change.

The Sinking Capital

More than 28 million people live in and around Jakarta. Its growing population and the effects of climate change are threatening its future as a livable city. It is sinking so quickly that as much as one-third of the city could be underwater by 2050. This is happening for several reasons. The enormous amount of water needed by Jakarta's citizens and industries is being taken from city **aquifers** at such a rate that the **water table** is shrinking, causing the land to sink. Rising ocean levels due to climate change also regularly cause flooding in the city, particularly during cyclone seasons. Swamps around the city are being drained to create more land for urban and industrial development. The government is proposing to build an entirely new capital city on the island of Borneo that could be completed by 2045. But not everyone in Jakarta can be moved to the new city. Many people wonder: what will happen to the millions who are left behind in Jakarta?

Flooding is a serious problem in Jakarta, causing buildings and roads to be submerged and often **displacing** thousands of people from their homes.

Around 40 percent of Jakarta lies below sea level—and the city is sinking lower each year. Some experts say that the northern part of Jakarta is sinking around 2 inches (4.9 cm) per year.

appeases Avoids conflict by meeting the demands of another

aquaculture Farming fish and other wildlife, usually for humans to eat

aquifers Underground layers of rock that can hold or transfer groundwater

archipelago A chain or group of islands in an area

aromatic Having a pleasant smell

cargo Goods carried by plane, ship, train, or truck

climate The usual, long-term weather conditions in a place

climate change A long-term change in the temperatures and weather patterns on Earth. Climate change often refers to global warming.

colonial empire A group of countries or colonies ruled by a single country or authority

colonizers Countries that take control of other countries or areas by occupying them

commercial Concerned with buying and selling

communal Belonging to or shared by all members of a community

Confucianism A way of life and worldview based on the teachings of Chinese philosopher Confucius

constitution A country's basic principles and laws

criminalized Made something criminal or illegal

cultivating Preparing and using land to grow crops

currency A system of money used in a country or region

deforestation Clearing wide areas of forest

delta A wetland formed where a river empties into a larger body of water

dialects Forms of a language that are spoken in a certain region

displacing Being forced to leave one's home

enact To make into a law

enlightenment Being enlightened, or gaining knowledge or understanding

enslave To take away people's rights and choice and force them to work without pay

erosion Gradually wearing away

ethnic groups Groups of people with common cultural backgrounds

exploit To use something or someone unfairly for one's own advantage

exports Goods sent to another country

extract To remove

fertile Land that is able to grow plants

greenhouse gas A gas, such as carbon dioxide, that traps heat in Earth's atmosphere

Indigenous The first inhabitants of a place

industrial park An area of land outside of a town or city that is used for factories and other businesses

industrialized Changed from mostly agricultural to more industrial

informal settlements Groups of houses, often crowded and makeshift, illegally constructed on public land. People living in informal settlements are often forced there due to a lack of affordable housing or after losing their homes in events such as natural disasters.

infrastructure The systems and services that help a society operate, such as roads and power plants

mandates Official orders

maritime Related to the sea

mechanization The process of introducing machines into a process that is usually done by hand

native Naturally existing in a certain place

originated Began

permits Official documents that allow something to happen

Persia A region in southwest Asia that is modern-day Iran

plains Large areas of flat land with few or no trees

plantation A large farm on which crops are grown for profit

port A town or city on a coast where ships can load and unload cargo

reincarnated Born again in another body

remote Located away from towns and villages

sparsely Thinly scattered

sustainably Used in a way that does not deplete natural resources or cause significant environmental damage, allowing for use in the future

terrace A flat area with sloped sides

textiles Cloths or woven fabrics

topography The natural surface features of land, such as mountains and valleys

tropical Relating to the areas on Earth closest to the equator, where the climate is hot and humid

tsunamis Series of huge waves caused by a disturbance in Earth's crust, such as an earthquake or volcano, under the sea

typhoons Large tropical storms that have violent, circular winds

uninhabited Not lived in by people

urbanization The process through which an area changes from mostly rural to more urban, with more cities

vulnerable More easily attacked or damaged

water table The underground boundary between soil and the area where groundwater appears

wood veneers Thin slivers of wood that are glued on top of a surface

Books

Auld, Mary. *Pathways Through Asia*. Crabtree Publishing, 2020.

Phillips, Douglas A. *Indonesia* (Modern World Nations). Chelsea House Publishing, 2005.

Reusser, Kayleen. *Recipe and Craft Guide to Indonesia*. Mitchell Lane Publishers, 2010.

Yomtov, Nei. *Indonesia* (Enchantment of the World). Children's Press, 2015.

Websites

https://www.kids-world-travel-guide.com/indonesia-facts.html
Check out these fun facts about Indonesian food, people, landscapes, the economy, and more.

https://www.cia.gov/the-world-factbook/countries/indonesia/
A detailed look at Indonesia—from its geography and people to the environment, government, and economy.

https://artsandculture.google.com/project/indonesian-puppetry
Explore the information, pictures, and links at this page to learn all you need to know about wayang shadow puppets.

https://artsandculture.google.com/project/wonders-of-indonesia
Learn about the many cultural treasures of Indonesia.

About the Author

Linda Barghoorn has written thirty children's books for which she studied a wide range of topics, from deserts and earthquakes to refugees, resilient cities, and remarkable people. She is an avid learner, explorer, and traveler. When she's not at work, she can most often be found hiking or curled up with a good book.